In *PearlStitch*, Petra Kuppers initiates us in ritual conversation, collective and intimate. Her embodied engagement with the political, mythical, pop cultural, feminist, historical and scientific brings poetics into the commons all the way through to the tender touch of lovers—knitting labor with Eros, "beneath your fingers, worker, is your fantasy and your redemption, meet my eyes, beloved,/turn around." These are incantatory poems, stitching together (the purl of) factory floors, canopies, rivers, borders, sidewalks and streets. Invocations of singer Madonna, Beatrice and Sophia converge with Jung, Wittig and Audre Lorde. Kuppers contends with systemic violence as in the murder of women in Júarez, Mexico and the ravages of neoliberal capitalisms, while also bringing the sensate, individual body into presence on the page, in alchemical discovery and in pain. She traces our own proprioceptive map of chronicity, a million tiny stabbing decrepitudes, "spines protruding into the melody's gap./Glottal rhythm hiccup and veering off downward and out." At the same time, and throughout, she dances in solidarity with queer and disability activists toward the possibilities of relational healing.

DENISE LETO and AMBER DIPIETRA

A pearl stitch is a chain stitch, also known as the basque knot. In this garlandy chain of poems, Petra Kuppers interknits a mythology of heroines, natural wonders, marvelously slippery identities, personal struggles and exultations, but also acknowledges the violence by which text-making and life-making takes place in our world, whereby the "endless piston that drives the needle into the skin," looping and connecting, is also the mechanism of our most elaborate cultural efflorescence. A beautiful meditation on the labor of making at all levels, *PearlStitch* stabs out a love letter to the love that fuels our creative surges in spite of all urges toward its perversion '

MARIA DAMON

PEARLSTITCH

PearlStitch
Petra Kuppers

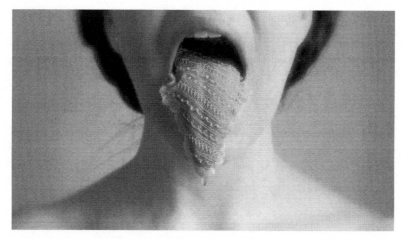

SPUYTEN DUYVIL
New York City

ISBN 978-1-944682-06-4

Cover Image: April Dauscha: *Custody of the Tongue (veiling)*, video still, 2013.

Image Description: The lower half of a white woman's face, with her tongue sticking out, and a delicate lace stocking over her wet tongue, dripping. The black hole of the throat leads the eye into depth.

For Stephanie, with love

To the pasts and futures of feminism

To factory workers

To the disability activists of Arnieville

In memory of vanished women

TABLE OF CONTENTS

Hagiography

Sophia: the mother of wisdom, the patron saint of alchemists. Jehova's grandmother.

Orphea: Monique Wittig's singer who pulls her dead lover successfully from the Underworld.

Madonna: pop icon, elusive object of desire in Desperately Seeking Susan. Also Virgin with large mantle for all mankind to shelter in.

Hermes: messenger of the gods, with winged feet, sly, swift, personifies alchemical knowledge. Roman name: Mercurius, gives his name to the philosophical mercury, quicksilver, the substance that puts alchemical processes into gear.

Beatrice Portinari: Florentine gentlewoman, Dante's muse, his guide through paradise in the Divine Comedy.

Mother Ann Lee: founder of the religious orders of the Shakers. Disapproved of sex, thought the Shakers should multiply through conversion. Shaking as prayer.

Olivia Newton John: a muse on skates, trying to enter Los Angeles and the (love) lives of mortals, ends up being a waitress.

LABORATORY

The journey begins, young one.

The journey starts here, initiate.

The journey, again: through the celestial spheres, carry what you can, and see what changes.

Take this recumbent dragon's blood, Orphea, Hermetica, double witch, and mount the rings.
Name them. Parse them. Square the circle.
What will be left behind when you run the ancient score?

Io Saturnalia, festival of lead
heavy foot thump deep on asphalt street desert track
rain dark tannin pine nude dead

wait now for the whole.

Just wait, eat, drink, and fall into the gutters a yoyo, a dreidel, the carnival of flesh, abundance
shimmies around the hips
guttural moans as you heave it up with your servant as you bawl it out with the cats.

The sullied garment of the soul, oh pine

shrink bark and shoot against the heavy load.

The dead in the retort, dragon corpse, burnt in industrial fires.

The nucleus reclines darkly, tired, tired to the earth, the earth, so tired. Watch from the tiny
window hidden, ask yourself,
which servants do not get to swing it low which slaves have to sleep in the day?
Factory foremen let the office matron cut their ties from their throats.
The matron has fire in her eyes
Do you dream of the matron or the foreman? Or of the sewing wheel, other side of the seam,
endless piston that drives the needle into the skin?

What makes a model? Shape the clay and glass, puppet master when you dress, in the light, you pull on the history of women

whirr of the sewing machine in my grandmother's room made its way through the pine boards
the walls the floor and the duvet
listen to the hands and the eyes

factory floor waxed daily so you can skate on it

the casket of remnants: when no one is looking, you dive your hands right into the dark grove
feel suede and silk

uneven pieces scraped from the sides chemical glue smell
bones rendered down, ashes, the salt of form

in the production line, quick swipe, heave up, left, insert, smear as the plastic handle wedges
into place, wipe the glue, tuck the plastic, cut along the seam and discard the extra, be quick or
you burn.
Breathe, you, and me, and you, model, as we stand in our line our line our line the new smell
of cars and garments
warehouse smell autopsy boutique

beneath your fingers, worker, is your fantasy and your redemption, meet my eyes, beloved,
turn around
in the line turn around

Garment maker, border crosser,

tailoress of the clicking wheel, the tender button, stitch an armor of skin for yourself
wrap yourself in the softest microfibers your purple coat to shelter us
a thousand years and years have past.

Dead dragon skin lies tattered at your feet, resplendent one. Beloved nervous web,
you tapestry of light,

hide the rooms we knew nothing about, open the way.
What will you discard this time?

Dance in this dirt, let it rain

shine the skin tattooed with the maps of a country never yours, and claim it back
from the borders, from the earth from the aura outline of your form

fall shadow pool out and out

Dusk Space:

My hand a sea shore

reach out into the ocean of your world peninsula
invite the orca into its fjords

my soft dune, reach toward the cliff time ledge
in a tectonics of relation breathing globes of observation
your curve, the horizon beamed into space.

I press into your back

crystal spheres flow between continents reach to touch the watery mammal encompass your
soft breast
my hair slides against your throat rest on our darkening beach

Under Planetary Stars:

Your eyesight, clear brown and dark, pleated silk corona, hazel moon,

let me be the apple of your eye Eve's snake in the desert
as you wait for the dirty bus running like clockwork the tick of the machine still heavy in your
blood a wire needle tin and lead and the organs
drop precariously around your uterus your fingertips, wet dry and callused,
quick fingered crocodile tip snake traces left in sand

round shoulder brown braid
or gray one (when analyzed and segmented, fragmented, it shows the spread of

the lead in the bands of spikes of the desert machine) who runs chamois along the palm of
your hand the outer smoothness of your thigh
at night? the bus stops at the night shift station
fear (of the reptile, buried, code break) in the flexing sole of your foot

tired or alert

the end

Commons:

listen all the way to the end, whore, widow, gather your wood (well stacked, they laugh, there's plenty of it) in the men's domain, beg for the pig to disturb the roots.
What remains of my specific flesh translation
transhistorical transcultural transfantasy transitory trance
and then my eye falls shut.

No one talks about alchemy anymore

find a path from the specific to the universal loneliness to fulfillment
stone to stele

roots twining into forest, the last commons, oxygen exchange

in the alchemical universe, the soul has split into myriad of fragments, and each human
carries their fragment of this light.
The body that surrounds this light a prison, poison, shade the world is sick
where is my place of rest?

In order to heal the world, the Gnostic hero has to lead the soul's divine light through the
seven planetary spheres, outwards and upwards to its old heavenly home.
As a woman, what is home? My flesh and my soul?
What is community amongst women?

SATURN

Behold, in Saturn a Goddess lies.

Your stinking companion, Orphea, is full

grave worms, gravid with the slick oil spit of the tundra she cooks at New Year's Eve
lead boils into the form.

Lead liquid, slide into the cool water

heavy Cassandra, your form (leaching) beneath my fingers. Is this clover?
Is this clay?

Is this the ring of my one true love?
father tells me about this shape
mother is silent (around the patio table, backyard, I think I remember my grandmother, old
and big, a mountain woman, foremother, Matilde, patient and cooking, and do I recall your
voice at all? Did you foretell my future in this lump of cooling metal? Was it your spoon that
rescued the message from the pail? Matilde of the silent tribe, I remember the hot water scald-
ing the baby, kitchen accident, and the fear. Matilde dispensing, pharmakon, you recede too
far in my memory, your nourishment no words nothing to remember but the smell and tight
beneath the flower patterns of your kitchen dress). Every year, the same message

The cauldron splits: here she comes again

prima materia, mother eternal, heavy metal cloak for no Madonna, no virgin, no whore, the cadaver of the one who will run the race, anew.
Shake for your liberation, Ann Lee, out of the form out of the form out of the form

Here is your mission, should you choose to accept it:

Carry this corpse, gently, through the ancient circles, one by one, and watch it changing you, watch it watching you, watch yourself watching, watch as you change what you watch, woman, and leave Hermes far behind, three-blessed virgin; mother, crone, hermetic three-sullied thinker, feeler, soul; fiercely carry your charge towards the light.
Simmer the food on the stove small flaming out in the gas oven the two-step in the light:
'one must listen to her differently,' write Luce
Iriga ray

I need to hear your voice, sweet one I need to feel your footsteps
your wheels' path your snaking ways
traverse over my own breast. Show me the way
I will dry my armpit hair in the public toilet I will lie in the dirty tent at the street's side I will
skate to the muses with you.
Your voice is sweeter to me than the song of Saint Peter that growling swell over an opulent
grave
Gregorian chanting sets my neck hair on edge your voice is sweeter than Beatrice
up there in the gods in the outer theatre on the big screen open your coat to me
Sophia, guide me to her

guide me to the one who will reclaim her skin and her soul in the fire.

Sophia, let me lie with you, at night your skin is dark like the gorilla's,
and you sit patient on the sloping mountainside

your skin is light like the face of a young Rhesus monkey,

and you scream with delight in the tops of the trees your skin has the spots of a fawn,
and the bruises of too much bloodletting

be my mistress, Sophia, silent or screaming, let me swim in your lymph,
let me climb onto your perfect red blood cells, cuddle down in the hollowed out sphere
let me rest while I witness your transhuman membranes
there she is, she who fights outwards, towards the light she, the hero, will sing
oh my ears oh your flow oh Sophia,
let us see who will hear and who will answer.

TRANSIT

(from Vogue, February 17th, 2010)

New York Fashion Week, designers inspired

by the idea of workers in Mexican *maquiladoras* walking half-asleep to the factories in Juárez, after dressing in the dark.

conjuring the spirit world at yesterday afternoon's
knockout

show their haunting new muse
sleepwalks through Texan border towns in a shredded gown of brightly colored wildflowers
It seems only natural that she might pause,

trancelike

to tuck a few wayward desert blooms into her hair

en route to nowhere.

intricate hair ornaments like wrecked, dried flowers broken off in little places molded copper pieces that were burned

painted over pearlescent finish
"the color of insect wings . . . you know, that weird, strange green or purple

[cast]." hazy-eyed, pale-skinned girls

"like beautiful ghost versions of themselves."

JUPITER

Lead poisoning: Zinc protoporphyrin (ZPP) is a compound
found in red blood cells

when heme production is inhibited
by lead and/or by lack of iron.

Instead of incorpo rating a ferrous ion,
to form heme, Protoporphyrin IX, the immediate
pre cursor of heme, in
corpo rates a zinc ion, form
ing ZPP.

She is dead. She is dead.
The witch is dead.

In your arms, beloved, in your arms to arms
to the glass ceiling through the spheres
she is dead, wail with the old women wail at the mouth of the church
wail and let your spittle run down the grooves of your face your old face.
Render your garment.

Render it down to the bare fat

render the butter that melts in my mouth. Render onto the king.
Render in kind.

Reindeer shall propel you towards the sun She is dead.
I caress the sound of her muscular exhalation. Witness the corpse sweat gliding over cooling
skin. Your skin is clammy, beloved
Beloved, your skin is not yourself.

The pistons of your muscles no longer drive the platelets through the vein

no plasma roars through the caves of your heart metals sink
solids sink

my ear is attuned to the free fall of your matter, my beloved drying, and pooling, spreading.
Your buttocks melt out like wings

your back relaxes down into the earth's embrace

I watch your color change (the coffin in the nunnery, the old priest, flowers, lilies, rush away,
you and me, all eyes and fingers)
dissolve into a waxy blue

just beneath the surface of this skin this epidermal entry way
flowing delivery system of the tactile erogenous border zoning law past the bars
on the plaza

down the dark road from the factory outside the zoo
protozooic plasticity

the heave of foreign gases

Speed her on her way, messenger.

Cartilage of your ankle joint expanded into tumorous wings cellular lightness too fast
cells that reach far behind yourself do not wish to leave
behind

those who send you on your way Reaching back
you fly forward your feet bound
bound to the gravity of the scene that unfolds like feathers: here I am, I am,
and my arms are full,

and the blood that coursed through our pulsing lips

stilled into blue pools spreading from my one forearm to the next. All my arms are falling
asleep with the burden.
Take her.

I have to wait for this story's hero. Claim it back.
Claim back my love, claim her name,

make her name resound in the plaza, the papers.

Names may flow in the forest capillaries in the Mesopotamian veins of cork.
Should you choose this mission, spastic messiah
erotic daughter of Mother Ann Lee these names might creep up elder trunks
runic arbors for our willowy, oaken forms. I remain planted.
Is flesh material

the debris you build over, messenger, silver-witted one?
Multiply this transmutating flesh fat food for many,
winged ones, and crawling, slithering and scurrying, rent and dissolve,
fester and maul,

let there be multitudes at the carrion festival. The table is richly decked.
Spread through my salivary glands, past taste buds that dissolve this flesh

map its aromatic memories

sensations delicately affirm my breath

psychoactive chemicals transfuse through the chambers nebulous hormonal home
your scent remains on the pillow for years

my sweet, my sour, my tart, my bitterness, my meaty ocean salt.

He sticks his salty finger into my mouth

taste do not even scream, frozen
startle reflex like a fucking possum his meat on my teeth groping deeper why don't I bite down
now
shy not release the lioness the panther flesh-eating revenge goddess
no no frozen in the video room of the museum
(Alien's vagina dentata, my mouth does not clamp shut, Frankenwoman with invisible wires
where I can't feel them, feminist cock stranded shore flesh politics of too many
nudes) unequal to the trans-cultural transgression
skin color gender caught
what marks out the victim in the dark hollow of the cinema

daze gaze daze days
tactile cinema deep in my throat

In the juicy warmth of your disintegration, my beloved Beloved, I try to hold on to
form

remember these borders lands of the pasture
my garden Eden

form a new terra, here initiate
take your magic,

and I wait, wait, deep inside my eternal friend. Sophia shall rock me.
Here is my burden

flowing toxic in this blood. I bless you, young one.
I bless you and give you nourishment for your path no pure rinds
no manna

but the sweet flesh of my breasts.

MARS

The wheel is moved forward and back forward, forward and back again,
that is the particular

direction that is imparted in pressure waves pushes no curve.

Spokes, metal spokes,
spokes quite monstrous ordinarily, aligned to cascade into a point
a dragon's red tooth

The tensile steel is not necessary. The plastic will do as long as there is equal pressure and no
flex
there is no place that needs to bulge out to the side and veer inward.

What is the impetus that makes machinery that makes it thwack.

What is the impetus of the rolling line
and the necessary scar in the palm.
What is the impetus. What is red freedom what is it
where is the languid length

it is there and a dark place is not an open place only to walk away
to come back when wanted only perch with tense thighs a perch that is water
the muscle has no color. A line distinguishes it
In the newspaper, below the fold, A line break, just distinguish it

C4, T4

Fire in the hole. Brother
Sister

You have lain too long outside the gates of the kingdom
soldier queen bedding an endless row of kings.
Milk, and blood and the fats dissolving in the chemical heat new births, my dears, new births
under the smile of the moon under the sickle of our attack.
Your teeth stand

row upon row a shark's maw

no longer hens, ewes, no longer lionesses. Initiate, I greet you.
Claim back the beloved's bodies, for ourselves.

We stand, and sit, and lie down my hand resting on your foot your hand in mine
head on shoulder

we reach out: in the circle of the activist camp circular dignity
homeless

homemaker circular freedom of care
representation and power

dust upon your brow, beloved,

fight in the circle of the activist camp my arms, to arms,
through the fire

documentaries about maquiladoras factories on the silver screen
TV drama, LA Times, there's a ghost in the machine prays
cross solidarity from far away who can speak for her
which women find voice in our market place? Our greasy stories connect
wagon upon wagon

unknown goods push by on bucking trains circle the earth, one meadow at a time.
Mothers, lovers, where do we sit and stand together? (brother)
Ashes Ashes

We all fall down.

Maria breit den Mantel aus Maria spread your mantle wide
Mach Schirm und Schild für uns daraus Make screen and shield of it for us Lass uns darunter
sicher stehn
Let us stand safe beneath it Bis alle Stürm vorübergehn Till all storms have passed
Gracias Madre

Now you have pierced the storm cloud shred the membrane
slash the lions and tigers circle, knife in hand, lightly on your feet
full of the lightness honed to the blade
dance and duck, duck weave you remember rock'n'roll
in the rap gap of the knife edge rap trap
weave in and out of the light flash on your hair
then storm forward blood blood
for a long time

for a very long time there's the spray and the glow for a long time (brother) you stare at the sand
and the light leaks out and the rhythm these feet loose their wings
gravity as the goddess flees from the scene

from your feet to your knees

the vortex of the sun coils its last dragon breath your forehead moist on the gritty earth.

Stumble.

Asymmetrical lean away to alleviate inflammatory processes.

Spines protruding into the melody's gap.

Glottal rhythm hiccup and veering off downward and out.

Fingers out in the air one moment then in dense flesh, deep, kneading into soft tissue firmly closed into fascia shield.

Hitch in the line spreads into continuous erosion and depletion of cliff faces and crumbles hills, rolling dunes along the silk road, shift shift shift.

I cannot find comfort.

Behind the beat and my step is hesitant, lock hip into place and open my hand on the indigo flank a prayer of one more breath, one turn, one Calder mobile floating in the music's wind before smashing cold into the concrete.

I cannot get up.

Now music runs away on the toes of the sax shrilled oboe sliding brass tinned into ear and hollow behind my knee.

You are not in the hollow, or in the hand that cups bone and there is nothing, you are not there and no pillow.

Air does not insulate, no heat flows over into the contracted point, the straight razor articulating the bend in the joint, overshooting its target and hover hover over the sorenesses and my loss.

There is nothing.

Your hand shifts into alien country. A bar on a rogue red planet. The rules are lost, deeply buried in sand and crystals despair unmet passing ghost on the other side of the mountain.

Music ends.

Sun water mercury acid sulfur iron oxygen copper

you built yourself a circle home in the desert, from grains of sand, you've hidden yourself.
I walk through the desert wailing, I walk to call for you

there's camels and carpets, and silk and bells, but then they vanish, and the street is baked
hard and red clay.
I still call for you in the desert. It is time to change our location. Let us leave this trap.

and i and my body rise/with the dusky beasts/with eve and her brother /to gasp in /the unsub-
stantial air /and evenly begin the long /slide out of paradise /all life is life. /all clay is kin and
kin. ----
                                                                            Lucille Clifton

VENUS

'one must listen to her differently' Oh Luce Oh Iris Oh radiant Oh g(ar)ay Oh ray Oh Lucia Sophia Audre Beatrice TaO Matilde Gertrude

The breath is the beloved

The breath is the beloved and I welcome you

and I speak with the breath beloved I speak and I welcome you

My breath and my flesh and I need to repeat it,

repeat it, again, and my breath and my flesh is the beloved and it is me and I welcome you

And I dance with you and the breath and what I call air when it is not inside me Beloved
I welcome you Beloved
In the grace of my air

In the grace of my flesh pain textures of pain I greet you and welcome you
My beloved

I welcome you

Earth ancestress, Fourth term, once the most fertile, Beloved, breath,

I welcome you

My world, in which Bobby Ewing can come back from the dead just by taking a shower, an invagination in the wetness of the TV,

this medium the message of hot and cold prickling pears my bare back a wide double bass?

my organ, which is not *an* organ, is counted as no organ so sing
the flesh is the beloved and I welcome you
and I dance and move this weight and this skin sings and the flesh is the beloved and I wel-
come you

two lips embrace continually so it sounds:
from dullness into the light, and I breathe into the comforter, alone in the night

The dragons come with their fires and steam, I want
this fluid embryonic feeling

let me ceaselessly embrace these words

reeling in the embrace of a gravity that hollows me right down

to the arching back, to the sustainment of motion as my hands and elbows find Tai-Chi false
memory
and my knees, tenderly, bob and test out motion

The flesh is the beloved

and I dance and move this weight and this skin sings and the flesh is the beloved and I welcome you

The breath is the beloved and I welcome you

and I speak with the breath beloved I speak and I welcome you

Fire smell in your hair.

I am your shark, he sings, my foot voracious, burning in my joint as you open up, twist into the elegant crease of your waist, turn, curls flying, step right back into my arms' closure.

I am your heart your shark.

The steps vanish beneath me as the violin drifts up my spine.

My hand planted beneath your shoulder blade, a firm stone against the velvet. I migrate across vertical plane and rock.

One shelf, to the next, handhold in the precarious stumble of my poor knees, my back unsure of its bend.

My cheek leans into yours in the suede of a rock-n-roll tiptoe, my cheekbone lands, a sliver open between our lips.

My feet march like they never do, driven between your legs, a firm twist onto the open ledge.

Accordion breath through the shoulder girdle. Leather straps reach backward. The lasso that tugs you, in time, into the beat, strikes me, the force of a boulder in its socket. Snaps shut.

My legs open wider as I step, again, free arm vibrating with the weight of your warmth, the heat of your palm driving down to connect me, mountains and all, to a rhythm that unzips my hips.

We sway. And then we move, glide, eyes closed, over the smooth wood, into the ascent.

Samsara suits me

A world that is full with images of itself

My question is one of prosody: what was the sound
Before the word that touched and broke the spheres' harmonies

Glass splinters raining down on the creation scene

The angel's trumpet already secondary, derivative,
Shivered into being
Sound being Safe being

Let me hear thy name

Search the deserts of the world

Clasp thyself in felt and fat and murmur to the coyote
Fall from the sky and dance

An empress in a bunny-suit, searching for a touching movement moment
In the swinging gondola over the abyss

Lament and let the pitch scale up and up till the glass breaks

Let me hear my name

How can trumpets build this city on rock-n-roll?

Fully paid up, I can experience the ecstasies of sound healing right up close, dreadlocked beauty, the shaking sweat,
he does lull me, my bones open to the sky and the rain Dooo yoooou feeeel theeee beeee-looooov(ed)?
Oh didgeridoo

> I do not remember, but my bones did respond,
> I think, lifted out of this flesh,
> pink bones full of blood and alive,
>
> pulsed, for a moment, into a canopy for me,
> a personal sphere, expensive crystal, wedding dowry, all these images getting in the way

that sound moment, honest, a time ago, an eon, last week?, let's do it again, save up and drive, and be careful on the cliffs, and do not fall over, now, will you.
Do not fall over Do not fall

MERCURY

Let's live in a Steiner house, edges round
no angles saturated in color
glazed, in complex patterns, jeweled walls to code my life
Is it my blue phase?
Colors are stardust. Minerals cooled with the core. Iron is red, copper blue, and sulfur yellow.

Nervous system, nervously wriggling just next to my skin, so hungry for the Vitamin D, which
is how I think of sunlight, of course: it's good for me, right now, in moderation. I will monitor.
Blue.

Or orange. In the bathroom

Koyaanisqatsi 'a state of life that calls for another way of living'
Builders are so expensive these days.
It's the recession, a regression,
a doom for the exploitation of the earth: mined out, leaching,
red and white scars where the soil shifts.

Lemon yellow:

the sour, and astringent, pulling it together, all together now, it's the nesting idea: we live in insecure times.

Let's live in a Steiner house,

One here and one there, and no edges. Organically, I fall all over myself to get to the sun I hide in the cellar
my head pounds. Eyes fall out.
Eyes grow hollow.

The back of the neck far away from the forehead that screams pinched from above and pulled and
the bed offers not enough black.

Paint the world black behind your eyelids. Blackness creeping over the world.
Paint black the room and the city and this strip of land and the snow and the river and the whole of the US and the earth and the round marble in space and space, and space itself, and the spaces between space
and then there is black to be painted and space is black.

In this dark alley, my knee locks panic breath
hitch in the air

Breath pattern

wink of bone against bone: hear the grating breathe against or with
patterns of resistance, pearlescent flow

Kugel: round bone head rotate inwards, into the mountains balance on the crag's edge
grind cracks as the circle sinks

so lift: breathe diaphragm blooms lengthen tendon
complex picture paints in blood and sinew stitches a band-aid across the site

a brick is a brick is a brick crumbles free under my hand
lift the Kugel (bowling ball with too many cracks, use value negligible, too smooth so smooth
never cavern no)

ravenous maw that cuts into curve balance on the needle
one breath, and it falls: sword bite
bowling alley limp that knee up, up and freeze: breathe.
a breath is a breath is a breath

If you want to get away, if you want to roll and fall and start again, breathe
this round volume of the lung, my aviolae balls in mimicry to live, to heave.
Measure the curvature,

correspondence, despondence, dependence secure round of the bone ball,
bone cradle call you, you, you, into the round respond, wave of compression
circle wheeling wheezing: breathe

In this dark alley with its smell of piss and garbage my knee locks
me out out
breathe out

breathe in breathe out

in the dark alley breathe in and out and breathe

and the word shall open the gate

and the word shall soothe the sand

and the word shall harbor the tree

and the word shall water the seal

and the word shall dive for the whale

and the word shall stem my cells

and the word shall crack the code

and the word shall laser the debris

and the word shall lay claim

and the word shall have dominion

and the word shall free my blood

and the word shall ice the fire

and the word shall cool my brow

and the word shall undo my fear

and pain will be erased

and pain will be destroyed

and pain will be conquered

and pain will have no place to hide

and pain will whimper inside

and pain will be heard no more in this land

MOON AND SUN

Carl Jung describing a woodcut, The Mountain of the Adepts, Steffan Michelspacher, Cabala, 1654, in *Collected Works*, 1942/1968, 12: 295):
The temple of the wise ('House of Gathering" or of "Self-Collection"), lit by the sun and moon,
stands on the seven stages, surmounted by the phoenix.
The temple is hidden in the mountain

–   a hint that the philosophers' stone lies buried in the earth and must be extracted

and cleansed.

The zodiac in the background symbolizes the duration of the *opus*, while the four elements indicate wholeness.
In foreground, blindfolded man and the investigator who follows his natural instinct.

You laid down in the dirt of the desert, sweet one, pear,
peach,

strawberry hidden in the soil cherry with the hard stone melon
plum

apple of temptation adam's apple
apple of my eye potato in the ground
wide spreading, engulfing root system

rhizome of abundance and scarcity, skin stretched open, thirsty to seal in each droplet of
moisture
eyeing up your tatters smoothness of your skin
keloid across the wrist and near your temples

ripe juicy ribs ribbon tips lacy vein venal arterial flower spray cinema of peeping tom

more likely, you have your nap and go home and go to the factory again tomorrow and home and the factory and the young man and the young woman and the child and home and the post office and the factory and home

You go to a shoot and a rehearsal and a shoot and a casting party and the couch is just there for you to park your cute behind and home and bed and tea and the street and the make-up

The piano player plays with the stethoscope pressed to her chest. The piano heaves into its first sigh.

She monitors herself.

Behind her, rows of audiences swell into her back, breath pushing forward and back, and her heart is pressed.

The hammer sinks, felt muffles the clear line, and she attacks with all the fingers of her hand.

Waves of oxygenated blood travel down the paths of her breasts, fine capillaries suffusing tender tissue.

I can see her nipples lifting up to me, across the chair arm's hard divide. The feel of these delicate stems in my mouth draws water.

My tongue circles and the breath sucks inward, a gentle pull on rose skin, her breath above me thrown backward, throat exposed.

There is heat, and then the violin pulses into the piano's sound, drawn on the horsehair string, swinging wildly into the orchestral space.

Contained. Open.

The rhythm accelerates slowly, as the sound of breath and heart mount in the riffs of red-lacquered fingertips and the sideways pull of a tender wrist.

Two dark heads of hair, one silvered, dip like swans at the fall's beginning, a low curve into darkening water.

Her hand wanders deep into mine. Palms align into touch.

Heat.

Heat swirls out from the uniqueness of her rills and valleys. Land.
My own desert land.

My shadows melt into the orange evening sun. Wings unfurl into night sails.

They go up and down and up and down and we turn wheels turn
spherical revolution long cycle
cycle cycle
cyclical revolution evolution radical radix the still point of the turning reach out to touch the
skin as it passes by
the sound of the other smell of skin
sun burns down on my nape nape wings fly to you
flare to you like a bull protector crown me
yoke me parallel furrows

Invagination implies a confusion about the side you are on.

Which team do you play for and what about the organs?
The heart

is more or less in the middle

you know, and you only hear it louder on one side because there is more
for it to resonate with, the lungs wrapped lobular
around the action-packed muscle in its sac.

Metabolic acts lose direction

stuff gets shuttled aside into wastelands I have to make the best of it.
Layer around the irritation, help me,

lay and lay and lay till the light breaks on us in the morning. Pearl shift in the hollow warmth.
Trash art, found object sculptures,

your exquisite corpse unfolds before me.

Never mind the old crystal image feel it now,
as we get old together,

this translucent sacrificial dagger sawing away at the membrane.

Inflammatory responses attack the pollutant don't go away
help wouldn't hurt so much let me rephrase
let me speak with my liver

Bioremedial intervention requires the trans formation of the toxic element,
its ree
valuation and rein sertion into the hol istic organ
ism

with calculated press

ure, the illusion of control, the illusion of freedom of movement, authentic movement,
myself, my self, grind my own axe and corn, I herewith name you

Change gender

Change genus

Change somatic structure

Change your mind

just keep in motion

maybe it would be safer if you walked back, do not take the bus, avoid the public spaces
do not talk to strangers

keep your gender alive in the luminous image on the wall and above your bed
do not take the bus

do not breathe in the exhaust fumes do not become exhausted
look after yourself with this orange organ
the Gila Monster waits out in the sand let us look at what is in the closet let's have a party
wrap us in the softest fabrics

you, and me, and the model, the violinist, and the hero, a cast party with the director matron
foreman father mother sun
I am so sorry that I can't give you a recipe from my grandmother

pearl stitch cross lung
brightest cave, toward

breathe

the seam slips over the border

NOTES

Some of the material here is reworked, substituted, reconstituted and reshaped from other sources, including various alchemical texts, the fashion pages of the Los Angeles Times, quoting Vogue, *Tender Buttons* by Gertrude Stein, material from Monique Wittig's *The Lesbian Body*, quotes from Carl Jung, Audre Lorde, Gloria Anzaldúa, and Luce Irigaray. Some of it emerges from ekphrastic practices, tango to contemporary classical music concerts.

Some of these lines resurface from the 80s, when I was working as a shift worker at Fibrit, a German manufacturer of interior car doors and instrument panels. We assembled doors on huge machines in workgangs, plastic and metal shaped through heating, suction and glueing, our fingers right in there. Hour after hour, I would sing to myself.

During my childhood in Germany, some of my family members worked in large fabric factories, and my writing remembers playing at the base of giant mechanized looms, and delving into buckets of fabric remnants in order to get away with small items of pilferage, little icons, forbidden textures.

T4: the name of the euthanasia program run by the German Nazis, based on what they called 'the American Science.' The name is derived from the street name Tiergarten (animal garden). The Nazis used gas poison to kill over 200.000 disabled and ill people, perfecting a regime of gas chambers that would later be used in the extermination of Jews, Roma and Sinti, gay people and others.

Arnieville was an activist camp and tent village, created by a coalition of disabled, poor and homeless people, on a traffic island in a busy street in Berkeley, California, during May, June and July of 2010. People slept in tents three feet away from roaring traffic, fast wheels and exhaust fumes. Activists used their physical presence in these precarious and polluted surroundings, their art, song and a large papier-mâché puppet of Arnold Schwarzenegger, complete with raised hatchet, to protest the ongoing dismantling of the social welfare system. Much of this collection was recited in the tent village or written in response to the experience, and its politics were shared and discussed in the feminism/disability/poetry/performance research group that met at Arnieville.

Acknowledgements

Thanks to the San Francisco State University's Poetry Center and their Poetics of Healing series; the Subterranean Arthouse in Berkeley; and Playa in Oregon for their residency hospitality and companionship.

Thanks to the Institute for Research on Women and Gender at the University of Michigan, for funding my arts-based research project on feminism, poetry and disability, and all collaborators and participants in our workshops.

This material has been performed at Harbin Hot Springs and Bare Bones Butoh in California, at queer poetry readings and somatic performance workshops in Michigan, and at many performance happenings in the US, Europe and Australia. Thank you, all organizers and wayfarers in these great adventures.

I also want to thank and acknowledge the editors who have published segments in *Poets for Living Waters*, *Disability Studies Quarterly*, *Beauty is a Verb: New Poetics of Disability*, *textsound*, *Streetnotes*, *PANK*, *Epistemologies*, *Adrienne*, and *Sinister Wisdom*.

Lastly, thanks to all who make up my world, and the collaborators and friends in writing worlds, in particular Beth Currans, Denise Leto, Amber DiPietra, Eleni Stecopoulos, Megan Levad, Meg Noodin, Rob Halpern, Larry La Fontain, Georgina Kleege, Anne Finger, Katherine Sherwood, Margit Galanter, Marissa Perel, Kathy Westwater, Devora Neumark, Sharon Siskin, Anita Gonzalez, Carrie Sandahl, Aimee Cox, Jennifer Bartlett, Michael Northen, Sheila Black, Laura Hershey, Leroy Moore, Neil Marcus, Kaite O'Reilly, Shannon Walton, Becca Manery, all the participants of the *Movement, Somatics and Writing Symposium*, and Stephanie.

PETRA KUPPERS is a disability culture activist, a community performance artist, and a Professor at the University of Michigan. She directs the Olimpias, an international disability culture performance collective. She lives in Ann Arbor with her partner and collaborator Stephanie Heit.

58481745R00075

Made in the USA
Charleston, SC
11 July 2016